THIS BUSINESS ANALYST'S NOTEBOOK JOURNAL BELONGS TO:

_____

_____

_____

_____

_____

_____

✶

OBJECTIVE

PROJECT

✶ ✶ ✶

www.ingramcontent.com/pod-product-compliance
Lightning Source LLC
Chambersburg PA
CBHW051244050326
40689CB00007B/1059